Social Security
Behind the Scenes

Vanessa Ann Bates

PAGE PUBLISHING, INC.
Conneaut Lake, PA

First originally published by Page Publishing 2020

ISBN 978-1-64701-216-8 (pbk)
ISBN 978-1-64701-217-5 (digital)

Printed in the United States of America

Contents

The Beneficiaries that Could Not Read

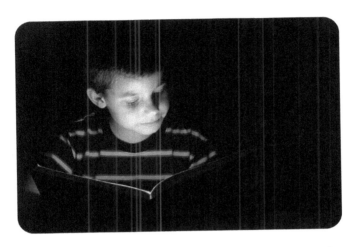

One day two rustic-looking men came into the Social Security Office asking for a replacement card. I advised them the application is on the counter, to fill it out, and that I would process their request.

They replied, "Ma'am, I can't read in the daytime because I went to night school!"

They could not read or write and made a joke.

I filled the application out for them.

Many people in the baby boomer era cannot read or write. Therefore, the representative had to complete applications for them.

The Drunk

In my position as a Contact Representative with Social Security Administration I met people from all walks of life, from training all world officials to enumerate all countries citizens, ambassadors, bank CEO's to the local drunk on the street. A drunk came into the office and told the Claim Representative, if you get me social security benefits, I promise you I will drink no more than a FIFTH a day. He was going to get toast every day.

Mentally Ill Beneficiaries

Later a mentally ill person came and asked me to help them. The lobby was full of people.

I asked, "How may I help you?"

He pulled a knife out on me and knocked my computer off the counter, which just missed from landing on my feet.

The security guard saw and wrestled him down to the floor. What a struggle—mentally ill people are strong. I took out running, what I do best. The guard was able to get the knife from the recipient and apprehend. A sarcastic employee asked me, "What did you do in the commotion?"

I looked at him and said, "I said to my feet, 'Feet, don't fail me now!'"

There were many people with mental disabilities that would come into the social security office that I was a victim. I even advised the security guard to hide her stick before someone come in and beat the hell out of us with the stick. Most of the offices were in the ghetto, and when there was a commotion, a shooting, or a mentally ill person fighting us, the police sometimes won't show or come.

There are many hurtful stories in social security. These are a few.

The Little Girl that Suffered Incest

A lady came in the office nervous, with her two children. I noticed the little girl was about five years old with a big-girl haircut. I asked her why she gave her baby girl a big-girl haircut.

She said, "We are suffering from incest. My daughter is so nervous that her hair will fall out. My husband want to have sex with our baby girl, and he tracks us down by the social security number. The police has given us a case number and request for a new social security number to protect my daughter."

Not knowing all aspects of the job, I looked up in program operational manual on how to give a new number under police request for new identity protection. By the grace of God, I was able to find the law and assign a new number. This family has a new beginning.

The Office Personnel
Management Beneficiary Tax

VANESSA ANN BATES

An elderly couple came in the office seeking help. They were just put on the street. The Intervenue had just evicted them from their home. They worked for the federal government and did not know they had to pay taxes on their retirement. The law was at that time, if you received your pension in 3 years you were not tax liable because it was all the money you invested. If you go past three years, you received more than your investment and taxable. I contacted my friend, the liaison for their congressmen, informing her the situation and advising her they could pay the taxes in installment agreement. God is good; Those people did not lose their home.

Beneficiary Losing a Million-Dollar Home

Another case where an elderly woman came in the office on the verge of losing her home. This person owned a home in Georgetown, and the property would be paid off for three thousand dollars. She arranged for her mortgage to be paid from the bank account her direct deposit of social security payment deposited into. The bank where her social security benefits deposit closed. Therefore, her benefits returned to social security and suspended until we could get a better address to send payments. The payments were in suspense over a year. Some reason a lot of banks closed in the early 90s and we had to wait for beneficiaries to give new destination to send checks; whether home or new bank. Payments were put in suspense.

After reviewing the information on the computer, I found the payments suspended in the agency. It would take several days to release the payment, but we only had three hours. Therefore, I alerted the computer that I was issuing a critical payment to the lady and pay her mortgage with suspended benefits. We met the three-hour deadline.

Beneficiary Losing Life over $40

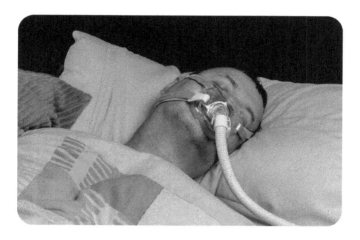

There was an undesirable, rustic-looking man that came into the office. No one wanted to help him because of his looks. He poured his heart out to me.

He said, "Ma'am, I'm going to lose my life for forty dollars. No one have $40 in my life. The electric company is cutting my electricity, and I'm on a respirator. When they terminate service, I'll die."

I reviewed his record and noticed the agency owed him forty dollars. He was on Medicaid, and they had paid his Medicare bill. Somehow the payment was in suspense, and it would take thirty days to issue payment. Therefore, I contacted the electric office advising the situation, pleading for two days to issue the critical payment since it was the end of business day.

The next day he came back, and I alerted headquarters through the computer that I was issuing a critical payment of $40 to save this man's life. His life was saved, payment issued, and the electric company continued his services.

The Apartheid

This beautiful, intelligent lady came in the social security office seeking help to receive benefits. It had been ten years since her husband died in the apartheid in Africa. She said the country is so behind it took five years to receive a death certificate. She went on to say she was a citizen from New Jersey and her husband was African. She had two children, and they followed her husband home to South Africa. She went to the American Embassy and filed a claim for benefits. And I saw on the computer we owed her $64,000 in back benefits.

I wrote Social Security International Affairs Department to release payment. It took thirty days, but the lady returned, saying she received payment and bought a house. Her children didn't have to be beaten by the apartheid because they are black; they are in America, where they can be free.

The Preacher Whose Taxes Were Filed Wrong

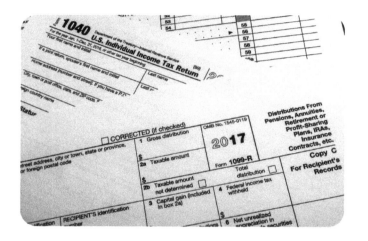

A minister had reached age sixty-five and came into the office to file for his retirement.

I said, "Let me bring up your earnings and send you back to the claims representative to file for benefits."

When I brought up his record, there were no earnings.

I said, "There are no earnings," and I checked if the earnings were filed under the wrong number. I said, "The only other reason is that your taxes were filed wrong."

He sent in his accountant for the past twenty years with his return.

I said, "You filed his return incorrect. You have to file amended returns."

It appeared he did not file the 941SE form for social security taxes to be filed with his return. The accountant got so angry with me because I advised the minister he destroyed his retirement that he got in my face screaming and his spat go on me I felt faint and had to pray to God to keep me conscious. It was the accountant error, he did not file the 941 SE form with the minister tax return.

Because it was the church, I discussed it with the claims representatives in the office trying to find a way to entitle him to benefits. He didn't want to file twenty years of amended returns; therefore, we could not entitle him. That was the first time a person spat on me, making me sick.

The Lady that Child Cashed Her Benefits

A liquor store owner came into the office with a letter from headquarters about him cashing two checks every month for a beneficiary. I asked him if he could bring the beneficiary in since he knew her to get a better understanding what was happening. He brought her in, and it appears that when the social security check showed in the mail, her daughter would cash her check and use it for herself. The lady would file for a duplicate pay stating the check was not received.

The liquor store owner was about to lose his license unless he paid back the overpayment in benefits. He was caught up in a domestic squabble.

I had the lady sign an agreement to pay back the overpayment in benefits in installment payments of what she could afford a month. It was wrong for her to file for payment when she knew what was happening. Of course, she could not fight her daughter, but she could report it to police as a forgery. She didn't want to press charges against her daughter. Therefore, the best solution was for her benefits to continue and pay the overpayment back in installments.

True Love

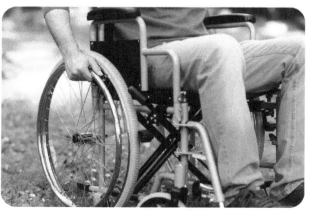

A lady came in needing an award letter for her adopted paraplegic son. The computers were down at the time. I told her I would give her a letter for Medicaid to pay his medical bills once the computer came back up. The lady loved her son and wanted him to have medical treatment. She prayed so hard that I was able to give her the letter within the hour. She went on to say the administration miscalculated his benefits and was going to cut off the little boy SSI check. She said they had so many expenses that she could not afford to repay.

I advised them that I would try to have the overpayment waived if she would bring in all their bills. I requested a waiver of overpayment documenting all expenses, proving the mistake was the administration's fault and they could not afford to repay. The waiver was granted! The little boy went home to be with the Lord. While he had breath, none of his checks were stopped or interrupted, and he and his mom never had to repay the miscalculated benefits.

I never knew anyone who loved someone so much and adopted a paraplegic and disabled child, love has no boundaries, you could feel this lady's love for the child in conversation. True love!

Adventures in the Field

The office would assign you positions and assignments out of your job description and categorize it under your job description: other duties as assigned. This was to keep you from being promoted or compensated for doing higher grade's work.

Often I would go out in the field with a partner seeking information to resolve post-entitlement problems with benefits. This was a dangerous position, acting as a field representative. We would go into Northeast and Southeast Washington, DC, ghetto advising people, beneficiaries, we were going to cut checks off or they owed the government $30,000 or $17,000 because of overpayment of benefits.

One place had sewage coming up from the basement and rats as big as cats running through there.

When I was walking down the street, a man came up to me saying, "Boat boat."

My partner said, "You don't need to be out here. He was trying to sell you LSD acid."

I thought he was talking about *The Love Boat* on TV.

There was a 4x4 truck going down the street with packs of dope on it. They were throwing packs of dope according to people's hand sign. Five fingers flash once $5 Flash twice $10 Fist $20. They had people on the ground collecting money. I did not know what it meant and my partner screamed, "Dope dope!"

I floored my car and got away. I wrote headquarters that it was life-threatening and too dangerous to go out in the field. I never had to go to homes in ghettos anymore!

My Gift to the United States Citizens

This is my gift to all mankind or US citizens. We would get alerts of possible death of social security beneficiaries with no death certificate. After investigation, the office said it was too costly to buy all those death certificates, and we didn't know what state they died in. My job was on the line. Therefore, I prayed, and God said, "Your Medicare—use your records."

When a person died, either in hospital or coroner records, it appeared that representative payees were all at one bank and nobody reported the death. The bank had millions of deceased benefits. I contacted Medicare Medical Record and was able to terminate beneficiaries' benefits with the date of death from medical records. After inputting this information, I collected $250,000. I contacted the Integrity Department with the information I discovered, and they were able to collect another $250,000. This is one of the reasons social security didn't go broke twenty years ago.

Hope you enjoyed these short stories about my experiences at Social Security.

Helped All Mankind but Could Help My Father

My father worked from age seven to seventy. His life dream was to retire and receive social security benefits.

My grandfather died when my father was two years old, and my father's mother died when he was seven years old. A neighbor took him in but put him to work caring lumber at the sawmill. My father only had a first-grade education. He could read three-letter words and count. My father overcame all diversities and opened a trash-removal business. When self-employed, you have to pay half of all employees' retirement besides your own.

When my father reached age sixty-five, he filed for his retirement; the law states that you have to sell and liquidate, or nothing to do with your business. No ownership! My father was holding the business for his children, who still wanted to own what he worked to have. The only thing he could do was wait until he was seventy years old and could receive benefits.

My father died on his seventieth birthday. My father never received a dime from social security. I could help all mankind, but I could not help my father, the man who carried trash on his back to rear me.

About the Author

The author graduated from DuVal Senior High School in 1973. She later attended Prince George's Community College, where she received a degree in accounting. The author went to the Office of Personnel Management for the Federal government and took the Civil Service exam, scoring 105 IQ. The Pentagon called her to work for the Army Discharge Review Board analyzing dishonorable soldiers' discharges for the Administrative Law Judges under the supervision of Colonel Dortch.

She continued her career with the Federal government at the Social Security Administration, where she was a contact representative. In this position, she was an advocate for Social Security beneficiaries interpreting social security, supplemental security, and Medicare laws, rules, and regulations to the public. She also was resolving any post-entitlement problems such as investigation lost benefits, termination of benefits, waiver of overpayments, and much more.

These stories took place while she was working in the government in 1977 through 1994.

The author finally ended her career as a Federal government worker and went home to the family business in private industry. There she became a certified minority business owner and service the Washington, D.C. area.

CPSIA information can be obtained
at www.ICGtesting.com
Printed in the USA
LVHW012308210420
654156LV00007B/530

9 781647 012168